What's in this book

This book belongs to

T0351529

_____

换牙了 The wobbly tooth

学习内容 Contents

沟通 Communication

数一至十
Count from one to ten

介绍年龄
Talk about one's age

生词 New words

★	一	one	★ 八	eight
★	二	two	★ 九	nine
★	三	three	★ 十	ten
★	四	four	十二	twelve
★	五	five	岁	year of age
★	六	six	牙	tooth
★	七	seven		

背景介绍：
图中的小朋友开始换牙了。

句式 Sentence patterns

六岁，我开始换牙。

I will begin to lose my milk teeth when I am six years old.

跨学科学习 Project

制作牙齿模型，温习数字

Make a dental model and revise the numbers

文化 Cultures

世界各地换牙习俗

Tooth traditions from around the world

参考答案：
1　I have 20 teeth.
2　I lost it at six/last month.
3　No, I have not, but she left me a present last time when she took my tooth from under my pillow.

Get ready

1 How many teeth do you have now?

2 When did you lose your first tooth?

3 Have you ever met the tooth fairy?

故事大意：
看看不同的小朋友在不同
的岁数都换了几颗牙。

liù suì
六岁

我们用"岁"来表达年龄，如
一岁、三岁、六岁等。

六岁，我开始换牙。

延伸知识：

儿童有 20 颗乳牙。乳牙通常的脱落时间：上下 4 颗中切牙为 6–7 岁，上下 4 颗侧切牙为 7–8 岁，上下 4 颗第一磨牙为 9–11 岁，下面 2 颗单尖牙为 9–12 岁，上面 2 颗单尖牙和上下 4 颗第二磨牙为 10–12 岁。另外，一般 10–12 岁将在单尖牙和第一磨牙间各长 4 颗第一双尖牙和第二双尖牙。有的人在 17–25 岁会长 1–4 颗第三磨牙（智齿）。成人有 28–32 颗恒牙。

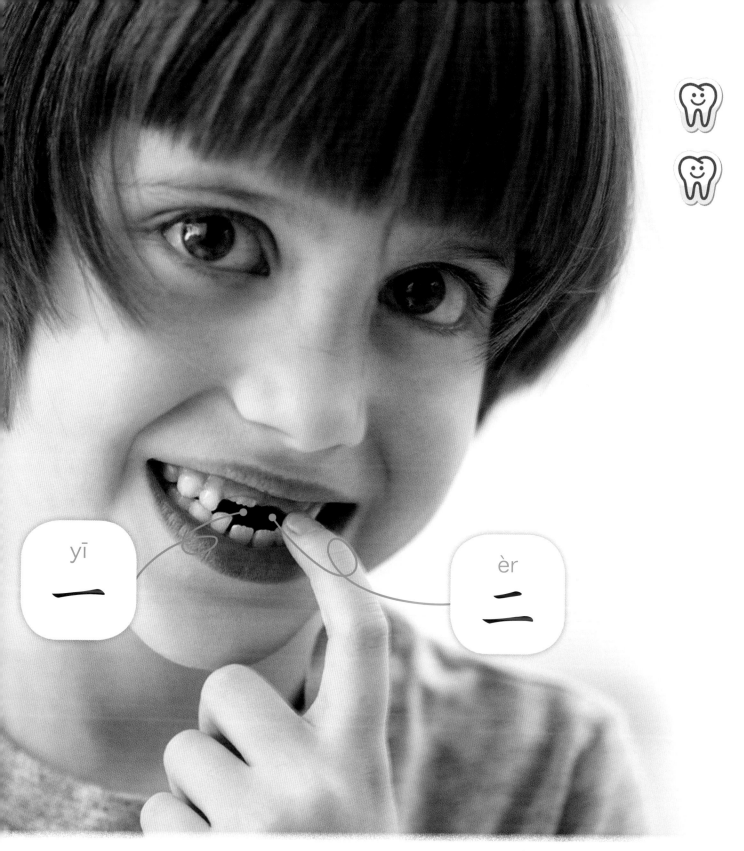

一 yī

二 èr

一颗牙，两颗牙。

提醒学生，在一般的量词前，以及说岁数的时候，用"两"不用"二"。如：两颗牙、两岁等。

参考问题和答案：

Look at the teeth on the right-hand side of this page. How many teeth has this girl lost?
(She has lost two teeth.)

七岁
qī suì

三
sān

四
sì

三颗牙，四颗牙。

参考问题和答案：
How many teeth has this boy lost? (He has lost four teeth.)

wǔ
五

liù
六

qī
七

bā
八

五颗、六颗、七颗、八颗……

参考问题和答案：

How many teeth has this girl lost? (She has lost eight teeth.)

jiǔ 九

shí
十

九颗牙，十颗牙。

参考问题和答案：
How many teeth has this boy lost? (He has lost ten teeth.)

shí èr suì

十二岁

告诉学生，数字"十一"至"十九"是由"十"分别与"一"至"九"这九位数字组合而成。

十二岁，我有二十颗新牙。

参考第4页延伸知识，提醒学生，到了12岁左右，除了20颗乳牙会全部脱落长出新牙，还会另外新长8颗牙齿。

Let's think

1 How many upper teeth of yours have fallen out so far?
Colour the teeth to show when they fell out.

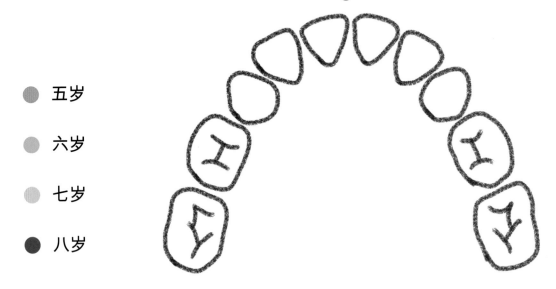

- 五岁
- 六岁
- 七岁
- 八岁

2 How do we keep our teeth healthy? Tick the correct ways.

a 经常吃糖对牙齿不好。

b 睡前刷牙是好习惯。 ✓

c 用牙齿咬铅笔的习惯不好。

d 定期看牙医有助牙齿健康。 ✓

New words

1 Learn the new words.

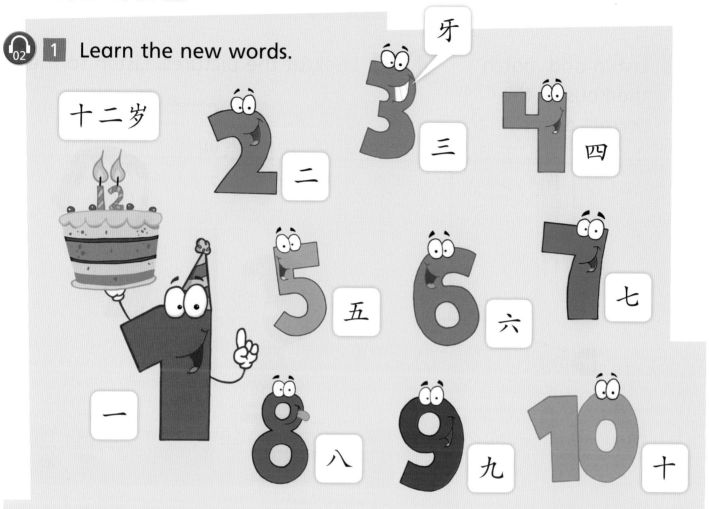

十二岁

牙

2 二

3 三

4 四

一

5 五

6 六

7 七

8 八

9 九

10 十

2 Join the numbers from one to ten and colour the picture.

让学生一边连线一边读数字。

听听说说 Listen and say

1 Listen and match the keys to the correct doors.

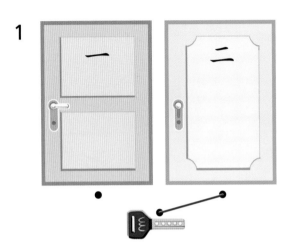

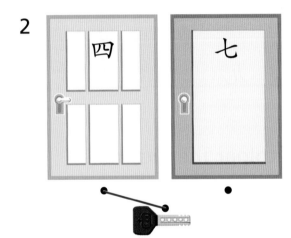

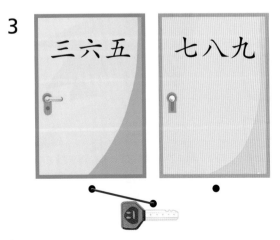

2 Look at the pictures. Listen to the sto

第二题参考问题和答案：

1 Where is Hao Hao? (He is at the dentist's/in the hospital.)

2 In Picture 2, how does Hao Hao look? (He looks nervous.)

3 Do you like going to the dentist's? Why? (Yes, I do. Because the dentist helps keep my teeth healthy./No, I do not. Because the dentists look scary.)

nd say.

一、二、三、四、五……

④ 谢谢！再见！

3 Tell your friend your phone number.

学生可先写出阿拉伯数字，再看着数字用中文读出。

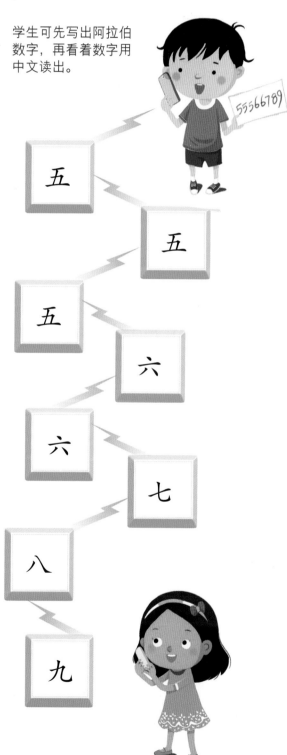

五
五
五
六
六
七
八
九

55566789

Task

Count the following items in your classroom. Write the numbers and say them in Chinese.

Game

提醒学生可以走直线，也可以走斜线。老师随后可跟学生一起统计哪条路线最健康（途经最多的牙刷牙膏和牙医）、哪条路线最不健康（途经最多的蛀牙和糖果）。

Play with your friend. Read the numbers to create a path from 'Start' to 'Finish' and ask the other to draw it.

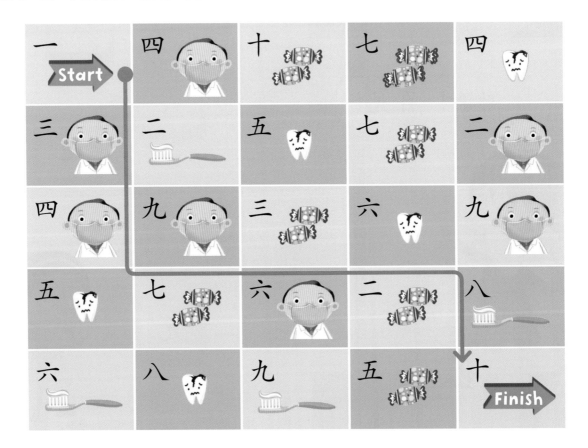

Song

老师可设定规则，使唱歌配合游戏进行。如：唱到偶数数字的时候女同学需拍手，奇数数字则男同学要站起来。

 Listen and sing.

一二三，三二一，

一二三四五六七，

八九十，十九八，

我有十颗小牙齿。

课堂用语 Classroom language

上学。

Go to school.

上课。

Class begins.

下课。

Class is over.

1 Learn and trace the stroke. 老师示范笔画动作，学生跟着做：右手在空中画出"捺"。

捺
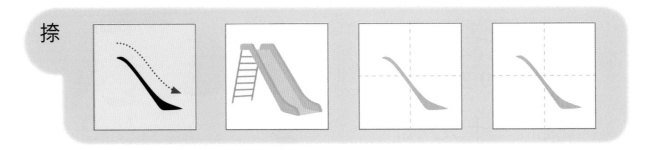

2 Learn the component. Circle 八 in the characters.

问问学生"八"像什么，并叫学生在自己的上唇上用两指做出"八"的形状。

3 How many 八 can you find in the Chinese garden? Circle them. 视情况提醒学生桥上、河里、树上、石头上和亭子上都有该部件。

4 Trace and write the character.

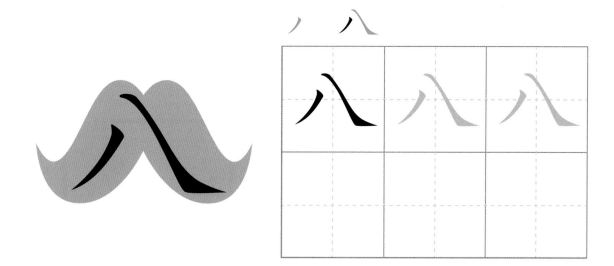

5 Write and say.

我 八 岁！

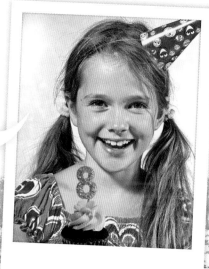

汉字小常识 Did you know?

Some characters are made up of only one component.

Read the characters.

一	八	人	五	女

该类型的汉字称为独体字。独体字是由笔画直接构成的汉字。

Cultures

Find out what children around the world do when they lose their teeth. Write the letters.

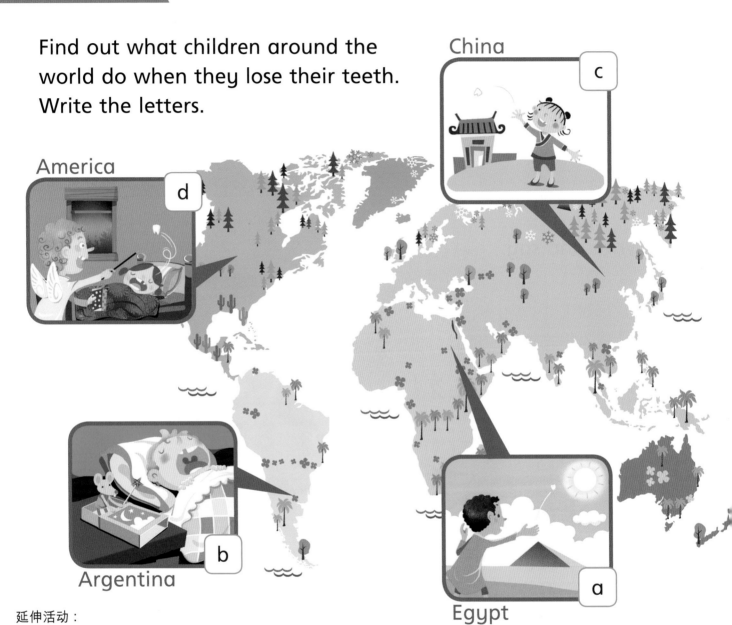

America

China

Argentina

Egypt

延伸活动：
学生互相分享自己国家的换牙习俗。

a	b	c	d
I throw my tooth towards the sun and the sun will send me a better one.	I put my tooth in a box. The tooth mouse will take it and leave me some money.	I place my upper tooth under the *bed* and my lower tooth on the roof. This way, my new teeth will grow healthily. 上牙丢床底寓意新牙顺利往下长，下牙丢屋顶寓意新牙顺利往上长。	I put my tooth under my pillow. The tooth fairy will take it and give me a present.

材料：四个六格的鸡蛋托盘、一张硬卡纸、一把剪刀、一瓶胶水。

1 Make a dental model. Learn to clean your teeth the right way.

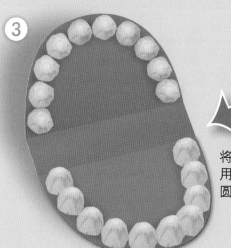

③

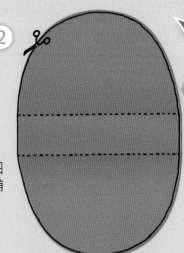

②

将鸡蛋托如图用胶水粘在椭圆形卡纸上。

从硬卡纸上剪出一个椭圆形，如图折出两道折线。再从鸡蛋托盘上剪出二十个鸡蛋托。

Brush and floss!

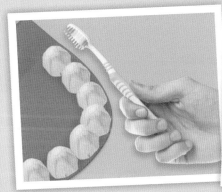

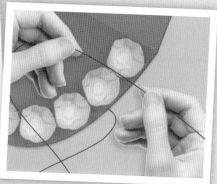

2 Count the number of teeth in the dental model.

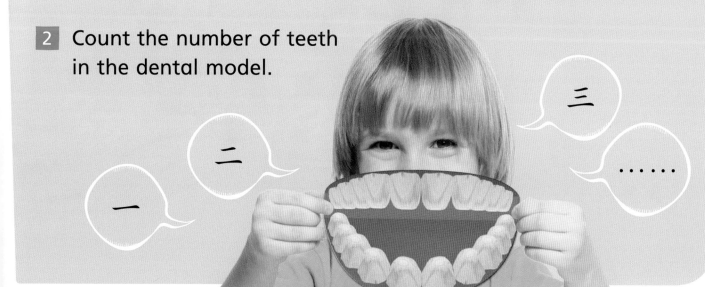

三

……

二

一

 温习 Checkpoint

游戏方法：

学生先在 Bingo 卡上写任意九个中文数字，然后圈出老师念的数字。当画的其中三个圈在横排、竖排或对角线上连成一条直线，即可举手并喊出"Bingo!"。最先喊出"Bingo!"的学生获胜。

1 Make bingo cards with Chinese numbers. Listen to your teacher. Who can get a row of three numbers first?

BINGO

九		
五	四	

BINGO

评核方法：
学生两人一组，互相考察评价表内单词和句子的听说读写。交际沟通部分由老师朗读要求，学生再互相对话。如果达到了某项技能要求，则用色笔将星星或小辣椒涂色。

2 # Work with your friend. Colour the stars and the chillies.

Words	说	读	写
一	☆	☆	☆
二	☆	☆	☆
三	☆	☆	☆
四	☆	☆	🌶
五	☆	☆	🌶
六	☆	☆	☆
七	☆	☆	🌶
八	☆	☆	☆
九	☆	☆	🌶
十	☆	☆	☆

Words and sentences	说	读	写
十二	☆	☆	☆
岁	☆	🌶	🌶
牙	☆	🌶	🌶
我六岁。	☆	🌶	🌶

Count from one to ten	☆
Talk about one's age	☆

3 # What does your teacher say?

评核建议：

根据学生课堂表现，分别给予"太棒了！(Excellent!)"、"不错！(Good!)"或"继续努力！(Work harder!)"的评价，再让学生圈出左侧对应的表情，以记录自己的学习情况。

My teacher says ...

分享 Sharing

延伸活动：
1 学生用手遮盖英文，读中文单词，并思考单词意思；
2 学生用手遮盖中文单词，看着英文说出对应的中文单词；
3 学生两人一组，尽量运用中文单词复述第4至第9页内容。

Words I remember

一	yī	one
二	èr	two
三	sān	three
四	sì	four
五	wǔ	five
六	liù	six
七	qī	seven
八	bā	eight
九	jiǔ	nine
十	shí	ten
十二	shí èr	twelve

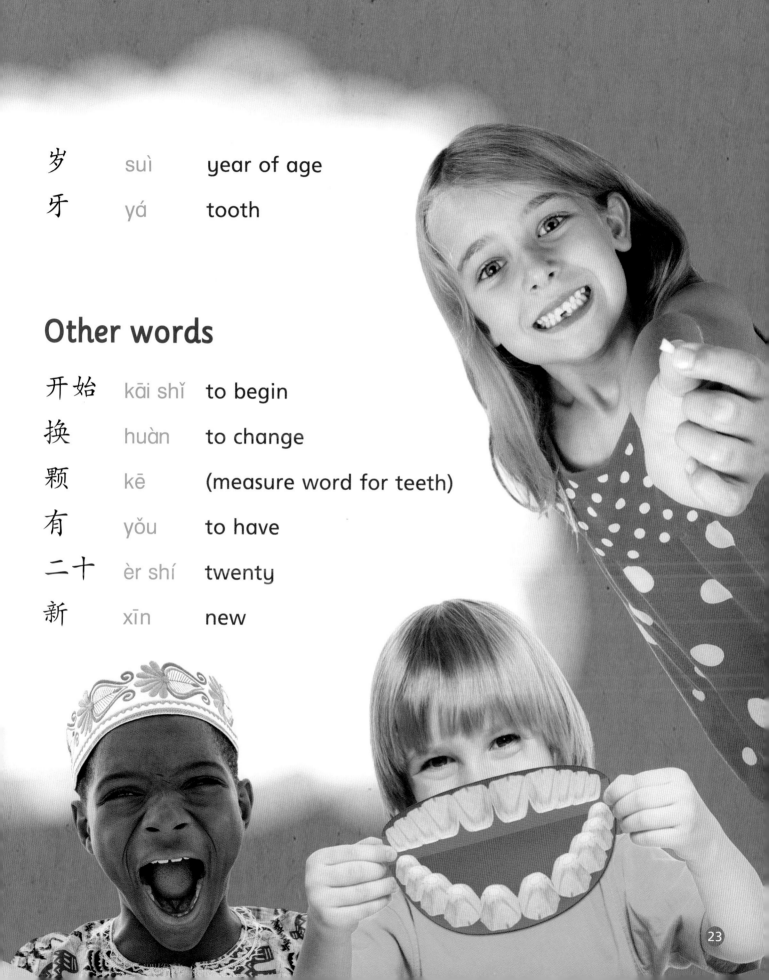

| 岁 | suì | year of age |
| 牙 | yá | tooth |

Other words

开始	kāi shǐ	to begin
换	huàn	to change
颗	kē	(measure word for teeth)
有	yǒu	to have
二十	èr shí	twenty
新	xīn	new

OXFORD
UNIVERSITY PRESS

Oxford University Press is a department of the University of Oxford.
It furthers the University's objective of excellence in research, scholarship,
and education by publishing worldwide. Oxford is a registered trade mark of
Oxford University Press in the UK and in certain other countries

Published in Hong Kong by
Oxford University Press (China) Limited
39th Floor, One Kowloon, 1 Wang Yuen Street, Kowloon Bay,
Hong Kong

Illustrated by Anne Lee and Wildman

Photographs for reproduction permitted by Dreamstime.com

China National Publications Import & Export (Group) Corporation is an authorized distributor of
Oxford Elementary Chinese.

Please contact content@cnpiec.com.cn or 86-10-65856782

ISBN: 978-0-19-942970-7

10 9 8 7 6 5 4 3 2

Teacher's Edition
ISBN: 978-0-19-082149-4

10 9 8 7 6 5 4 3 2